Acclaim for

The   Talking

"…great asset to parents… clear, straightforward, and easy to implement"

> — Barbara Billington-Smart, National Board Certified Teacher

"…delightfully written book, which offers parents a unique and valuable way of bonding with their baby"

> — Dr. Sandra Kagan, PHD Marriage, Family Child Therapist

"…a parent friendly guide that highlights language building opportunities in everyday child centered activities."

> — Marshall Fenig, M.A. CCC-SLP (Speech Language Pathologist), Med ECSC

"…this book is a keeper… a wonderful gift for prospective parents. When children can speak early, they can better express what they want, are less frustrated, happier, and more empowered… this early language development leads to an earlier readiness for reading and participation in the next developmental stages"

> — Roberta Corwin Robinson, M.A. (Marriage and Family Therapy), M.S. (Education, Specializing in Development and Remedial Learning)

"…a great source of information for any parent looking to help their child speak early"

> — Dr. Scott Aaron, M.D., Child and Adolescent Psychiatrist

"…wonderful tool for parents… very informative and enjoyable reading"

> — Nancy Johnson, Elementary School Teacher

"…fun and informative"

> — Dr. Rachel Kramer, M.D., Pediatrics Welcome!

See www.thetalkingbaby.com for additional acclaim/quotes

141533

The Talking Baby

THE TALKING BABY

by Jeremy & Kenna Sweet

simple tricks & techniques to encourage
your baby to speak sooner

Copyright © 2008, 2009

First Edition

ISBN 978-0-615-24382-5

Research, Concepts, Direction, Interviews, and Story by:

Jeremy A. Sweet

Karina V. Barinstein

Written Text by:

Jeremy A. Sweet

Illustrations by:

Kirby Shaw

Table of Contents

Welcome!

Being a parent can be one of the most amazing and wonderful adventures a person can experience. But it's not always easy. Sometimes the hardest part of being a new parent is not knowing what your little bundle wants or is trying to tell you. At this very moment, millions of moms and dads across the globe stare blankly at their screaming baby thinking, "What does this child want? Pleeeease, just tell me!"

And while the initial months will most likely be challenging due to a lack of communication, the constant searching for what your baby desires does not need to last long. Yes, certain children will take longer than others to start speaking, but through some simple techniques and guided encouragement, many children can gain the confidence and desire to speak sooner.

"Wouldn't it be great if little Sam could tell us he's hungry, wants his pacifier, craves an apple, thinks the bath is too cold, wishes to play with the puppy or ball, needs a glass of water, or simply wants more of something?" My wife and I watched countless friends and colleagues asking these and similar questions about their 7 month, 9 month, 12 month, 16 month, and 18 month olds. Fellow parents would look bewildered as our 1-year old would read off alphabet letters, name body parts, ask for cheese and yogurt, call for his sister, point to and exclaim "Buddha", or ask to watch Elmo. "How did you get your child to speak so fast? My 1½ year old just says 'dada'."

After enough of these comments and requests, we decided to share the secret. This book contains all of our research, studies, experiments, training and education simplified into an easy-to-follow guide to help your child communicate. As well, the techniques within can assist in bringing children up to speed who may be taking longer than normal to begin speaking. So since you made the choice to purchase our helpful manual, it's time to fill you in on the secrets to **The Talking Baby!**

A Happy Home

A happy home is a place where children will thrive. As an elementary school teacher, my wife learned early the importance of making the learning environment a happy and secure place. And in doing so, her classes were always the most sought-after by parents, rooms that principals continually exhibited to new teachers and visiting administrators, and places where children cried when they had to leave for summer vacation. As well, Mrs. Sweet's classes turned out many above grade level students.

After all, what child wants to spend half his waking day in an unhappy classroom, void of laughter, forced to listen to uninteresting lessons and stressed-out teachers? If this is the type of environment a child faces at school or at home, the joy and love of learning will suffer greatly.

Study after study have shown a range of learning difficulties and behavioral problems children can demonstrate coming from environments of abuse, neglect and negativity. Through the years as an educator, my wife continually observed this reoccurring pattern in classrooms: children with the greatest learning and communication issues often came from environments that did not nurture or encourage these youngsters. The children who excelled and had a thirst for learning most often came from happy and caring family atmospheres.

And while most parents are not intentionally hurtful or neglectful, they can unknowingly do things to instill frustration, withdrawal, or hinder a child's development and communication skills. They might excessively complain about each other in front of their child; they may promote a stressful environment by focusing too often on problems rather than solutions; they shout; they ignore; they do not forgive; they forget to laugh and play; they forget to love; they take out the frustrations of raising a child on each-other instead of supporting one another. You get the point. They take life too seriously and forget to create happiness in the home. So remember, while this all may seem obvious, happiness and security are key factors to raising a healthy, engaged and motivated child.

So, before you begin on the road to raising your young super-talking star, try to remember to make home a happy place. Minimize the stress your little one sees and experiences. Try to avoid petty arguments. Respect and love your family unit, however big or small, each and every day. And if parents must 'discuss' the various problems that will most definitely arise, find a time, space and volume away from your child's inquiring eyes and ears. And most of all, have fun with your little one(s)!   The atmosphere you create for your child, whether happy or stressful, can play a major role in how he or she takes to learning and talking.

With that being said, let's learn how to get that baby talking!

Cartoon Stew, Emotional Glue

Why does practically every kid love cartoons? How come Looney Tunes, Mickey Mouse, The Chipmunks, The Smurfs and other cartoon classics still remain so popular with children after so many years? And why are well-known toys packed with silly sounds, exaggerated voices, goofy noises, and other ridiculous elements?

Because they're attention magnets...visual and auditory stimulation sensations. Suppose you read a book in a slow, monotone, mellow pitch to a 1 year old (think Ben Stein's voice in Ferris Bueller's Day Off). This might be great for a hypnosis session or putting a baby to sleep, but it gets pretty old pretty fast when a little one is wide awake and wants stimulation. Stick a toddler in front of the Weather Channel and watch how fast she 'toddles away'. But flip on Sesame Street and notice her eyes glued to the tube. The same philosophy can be applied to how we can encourage our babies to speak or communicate.

Babies are fascinated by the world around them and are often switching attention, moods, needs, wants, feelings, and desires at the flip of a coin. Hysterical crying can turn into giggles, then back to tears, then back to laughing all within one minute. Little ones get easily frustrated and bored if they do not like something or are not having fun. Patience, control and a sense of 'the bigger picture' are not exactly a baby's (or some adult's) primary skill-set. So, how does a parent cope with this and teach baby to speak given a baby's lack of patience, limited attention span, and easy frustration?

Well, all your years of dedicated Saturday Morning cartoon watching as a youngster are finally going to pay off. All that early 'research' can now be put to good use. Now you are going to be your baby's favorite cartoon channel, as an important part of the teaching process is being able to keep and hold a baby's attention.

I always wondered why every child I knew got so excited to see and be near my mother. When my brother would bring his children around mom, everyone else in the room was suddenly yesterday's leftovers. My wife's mother had a similar appeal to the youngsters in her family. They just couldn't get enough of these grandmothers. Then it hit me one day (bonk!)...these women are walking cartoons. Their voices squeak in delight whenever they see their grandchildren; they constantly change pitch, volume, speed, and character when playing or talking with the little ones; they make silly sounds, exaggerated hand gestures, comical dances, and fun body movements just like many cartoon characters we used to watch and love. When they sing with the children, their voices crack in humorous, unintended and entertaining ways. And kids love it. Why watch cartoons when you have Grandma!

You'll find that this exaggerated, cartoon play approach will work wonders in teaching a child to speak. Like a cartoon, you'll need to be an attention magnet full of character, life, silliness and emotion. Psychological studies have found that people tend to better remember events that are associated with emotional experiences. Emotional experiences seem to be encoded in more detail in the brain. The thrills, feelings, and silly humor you add to the learning experience will become like glue, helping the material stick to your child's mind.

This is not to say that you need to be a non-stop, hyped-up, crazed, overbearing, screaming Tasmanian Devil when teaching your child. Cartoon characters, emotions, exaggeration, surprise and fun come in many shapes and sizes. Even tiny voices and silly whispers can do the trick. And while I'm sure you'll have some great ideas of your own, here are some helpful suggestions and examples to lay on that emotional cartoon glue and become your child's favorite attention magnet:

1. Teaching your little bundle to imitate fun **animal sounds** is a great way for baby to begin learning to speak. This is a perfect opportunity to really become a cartoon. Simply pointing to a picture and saying something like "The dog goes 'woof woof' may work eventually, but to really get baby motivated to say the sound faster, *add tons of emotion.*

Give him your best animated "MOOOOOOOOOOOOOO" or "MEOOOOOWWW" with a great big smile after saying the sound. Exaggerate and act out the animals sounds when showing a picture of the animal. If it's a cat, take a stuffed cat and nuzzle it against the baby while meooooowing. One of my wife's favorite things to do was to show pictures or toys of tigers and exclaim with a silly, fun exaggerated head shaking, paws extending, "Ra aaaaaaaaaaaaaaaaaaarrrrrr!" At first, our baby would laugh, but after no time, he was "raaaaaaring' with the best of them, thrilling pedestrians in book stores and local zoos! Make baby laugh at the crazy, silly and cartoony ways you act out the animal sounds, and he will want to join in the fun. Create the emotional glue.

2. **Learning Names** – For a baby to want to say someone's name, she usually needs to like that particular person and feel

excited in that person's presence. Parents can accelerate this bonding feeling, and as a result the want for baby to say that person's name, by creating a sense of excitement and emotion when that person appears. Say, for example, you are trying to teach baby her sister's name. Simply pointing to the sibling and saying the sibling's name may take a while to sink in and repeat back. But adding emotional elements can speed up the recognition and desire to say the name. You can have the sibling go to another room and make a couple fun noises so that baby hears the sibling. The parent might say "ooooohhhhh... what's that noise!???" After some more fun sounds, in an excited whisper, the parent might say, "I think it's Emma...[deep quick exaggerated breath in] ...Do you hear Emma? I think it's Emma. Let's go find Emma!" Sneak around with baby in hand like a cartoon looking for Emma. Help create the sense of mystery, excitement and anticipation. Let the baby peek around the wall to see Emma, and when she does, quickly pull her back and hide secretly laughing with her. Repeat this a few times, so that baby is in the cartoon experience and emotionally tied. Once the excitement has been built, fling into the room as if surprising Emma and exclaim "It's Emma!!!!...Emma!" Then give big smiles, kisses, hugs to show Emma is a trusted and secure friend. You get the picture.

3. Teaching the words **"up" and "down"** (helpful words for a baby to know). Pointing up and saying 'up' won't necessarily cut it. Instead, be a cartoon and create the emotions tied to the words. Take an object and in your funniest cartoon voice, say

"uuuuuuuuuuuuuppppp, up, up, up, up" as you raise the object into the air, then "dowwwwwwwwwn, down, down down" as you lower it. Make your voice playfully go up and down in pitch and volume as you show the object going up and down. Each time you pick your baby up or set him down, say the words and add the fun emotions ... "Up, up, up, uuuuup we go!" or "Down down

down, down...boink...onto the ground". In the bath, with a silly voice, show how objects go "down down down, dowwwwwwwwn" under the water, then "up up up up, up...tada!" as they spring out of the water. Always try to create the comedy and feelings to go with the words. Add your own crazy cartoon sounds and gestures to make the experiences emotion packed.

RECAP: Remember to pack in the emotion, wonder, and 'cartoon' into the learning experience. The more your baby feels the learning process, the sooner he or she will respond and want to talk. Above were just a few examples, but there are 1000's of fun, creative ideas. It might take a little more energy to act and create the emotion, but the payoff of having your child speak sooner is worth it, and will most likely save more energy and frustration in the long run.

Repetition, Repetition, Repetition

Location, location, location may be the key to real estate investing, but repetition, repetition, repetition is the key to baby talking. I can't even count the number of times my wife and I sang the ABC song or "Patty Cake". If I had a dollar for every "More?", "Peek-a-Boo!", "What Color?", "What's This?" and "Who's That?" my wife and I said...well, let's just say, money would be flowing in like water.

Familiarity and repetition ground a baby, helps her feel safe, and are key factors to instilling any lesson. Studies have shown that young children tend to like TV episodes and stories even more each time they view or read those same episodes/books. Unlike an adult who might become utterly bored watching something a forth time in a row, kids tend to behave in an opposite manner. They find security in patterns and familiarity. At first, to a baby, the world can be a gigantic, scary mishmash of constant unknown experiences and challenges. When they can grasp something familiar and recognizable, the world becomes less scary and more conceptual. Repetition will help create that security, and as a result, the confidence to begin speaking and interacting in this new and strange world.

There are no hard-fast rules as to how much repetition is enough. However, a rule-of-three is often useful. Instead of just saying "No", "Up", or "Dad", we've found it helps to sometimes triple the key learning word. This way, baby can hear how a key word is pronounced more than once, which reinforces it into memory. For example:

- "Tim, do you want to go Up?... Up? ...ok here Tim goes... Up Up Uuuuup! [parent lifts baby up in a fun way]
- "No?... Did Max say No?...ok... No No No!" [parent shakes head in an exaggerated way]
- "More?...Do you want More?... ok More!" [with excitement]

But remember to create the emotion as discussed in **Cartoon Stew, Emotional Glue**. Without emotion, fun, or interaction, it all just becomes a drilling of words...sometimes referred to as "drill kill." If a baby (or anyone for that matter) is bombarded and drilled constantly with words, void of any connection, interaction or space, the words can just be a rambling of annoying noises that the baby may tune out. As well, it's not so fun for a parent to be a non-stop tape recorder stuck on a robotic loop. Keep baby engaged and enjoying the experience. Interact with the words and pull back if you feel it's becoming "drill kill". We will see more helpful ways to keep baby engaged in future chapters (props, praise, singing, cueing techniques, senses, etc), but for now, it's good to understand that you are not simply drilling baby with repetitive noise. Rather you are using repetition to aid the recognition of words. Repetition is very useful, but more so when joined with multiple techniques.

Repetition throughout the day is also helpful. Singing the ABC song once a day is great, but singing it 5 to10 times a day is going to help get baby talking. As long as they are having fun and enjoying the process, go crazy with repeating a song, a word, or a sound. In later chapters, we will learn which words are easier for baby to begin saying, but words like 'No' and 'More' are very helpful in judging whether your baby is burnt out on learning at the moment or wants to continue the repetition game.

Once your baby begins saying words, remember to revisit and repeat those familiar words before encouraging baby to try a new word. Start with what they already know. As we learned, familiarity brings security and happiness to baby. The confidence, security, and praise babies receive in saying words or sounds they already know will inspire them to take on the next word. If baby knows how to say "Meoooooww" after "What does a kitty say?" …always start with "What does a kitty say….Meoooow (says baby followed by parent praise)" before jumping into the newest "What does a cow say? ….Moooooooo….Moooooooo."

Another important and obvious form of repetition is simply the act of talking to your baby. Parents are sometimes so happy that baby is not crying, for example while driving in the car, that they simply zone out and ignore baby the entire drive. There's a certain "don't rock the boat" fear that sometimes sets in with parents. It's completely fine to enjoy those quiet moments, but don't let them go for too long. Just because baby is not crying does not mean he is not curious or does not want to learn. When taking a walk with baby, remember to talk to baby and talk about words around him throughout the walk (e.g. – "trees ...what pretty trees! ...Oh, a ball, let's hold the ball! Can you bounce the ball?", etc.). As your baby is exposed to the world of speech, those sounds and words will resonate in him and help his talking experience.

RECAP: Repetition, Repetition, Repetition. Repetition allows for familiarity and security, which makes baby more confident and at ease to speak. Use the rule of three throughout the day. Revisit what baby already knows, and remember to talk to baby.

Praise Pays

An extremely important element in the talking process, and in raising a healthy child for that matter, is effective praise and encouragement. What your new baby needs is extreme praise...unbridled, hyper-enthused, standing ovation acclaim. When your little munchkin says those beginning sounds or words, it's time to get up on your feet, clap enthusiastically, smile, laugh and kiss like crazy. Make a fool of yourself. Make that child feel like a superstar, like she's just scaled Mount Everest and won the Nobel Peace Prize, all in the same day...at the age of one no less!

When your youngster has achieved saying a desired word or sound, even if not the exact right word or sound, follow the 3 "R's" rule: **Recognize**, **Reward**, and **Repeat**.

Recognize: Make sure to acknowledge the efforts made by baby. If your baby says or attempts to say a word, say the word back to baby and show him the object. Make baby know you are truly interested in what he said no matter how well it was spoken. "Did you just say Ball....Ball...yes, it's a Baaaaall?" Follow their lead and recognize what they are focusing on. Instead of only trying to teach them what you think is important at the moment, make sure to also recognize what they are interested in, reaching for, or wanting. You may choose to work on that particular word which is peeking baby's interest.

Reward: Rewards can be a number of things from claps, kisses, hugs, vocal 'hoorays' and 'yaaaaaays', to being able to play with, touch, hold or eat the object named by baby. Words like 'more', 'banana', 'oh' (the cereal), 'dog', 'apple', and 'ball' were early favorites of our baby boy to say as there were often tangible and pleasurable rewards associated with saying the words. But emotional rewards can be just as effective. Most babies are overjoyed by the smiles, tickles and kisses they receive from mommy or daddy as a result of their efforts.

Repeat: Always repeat the word back to baby... and try to have baby repeat the word again. The repetition will help baby focus closer on the enunciation of the word, and, as learned in *Repetition, Repetition, Repetition*, help them to feel grounded in this big and ever changing new world.

An example of a conversation using the 3 "R's" might go something like this: "Emily (deep breath in) what's this... what is this...? Is this a ball... can you say ball?", as dad bounces and plays with the ball. Suppose Emily repeats back "Ba" or even "ah". Follow this with "Yaaaaayyyy!!!" (smiles and clapping) [Recognize]..."here you go" as you let baby touch and hold ball [Reward]... Yes, it's a Baaaall... you said Ball! [Repeat].... Emily has a _____?..."

RECAP: All babies need constant praise and encouragement. Remember to use the three "R's" when teaching baby to speak: Recognize, Reward, and Repeat.

Vowels, Syllables, Sounds and Words To Begin

Before trying to impress friends and family by encouraging baby to repeat words like "Spectacular", "Kalamazoo" "and "Filibuster", let's focus on the vowels, syllables and sounds that are initially easiest for your pumpkin to pronounce. Studies have found that the explosion period of words usually happens once a baby has mastered some of the easier words and sounds. As with mastering most anything, it's important to first learn the basics, then build on those skills toward more complex goals. So while you want to continually expose baby (even during pregnancy) to an array of words, through

books, songs, etc. (discussed more in further chapters), it's helpful at the early speaking stages to put a little more weight on easier-to-say sounds to get the vocabulary ball rolling. Let your baby try out a 'white belt' before strapping on the ninja suit.

So what are these magic sounds and syllables? Most babies tend to initially and more easily form lip sounds (such as m and p) and back-of-tongue sounds (such as g and k). Through research, as well as in practice, we've found the following list of letters-sounds to have an easier 'early comfort zone' (we'll call "THE ZONE") for babies:

- **B** (as in ball), Hard **C** (' k as in Cat), **D** (as in Dog), Hard **G** (' g as in Go), **K** (as in Kitty), **M** (as in Mama), **N** (as in No), **P** (as in Papa), **W** (as in Want), and sometimes **H** (as in Hi)

- **Short and Long** 'O (as in 'Pop' and 'No'), Short 'A' (as in Dad),

Short and Long 'I' (as in 'It' and 'Bite'), Short 'U' (as in Up), and sometimes **Short and Long "E"** (e, é – as in 'Pet' and 'Bee')

We've also found the more difficult letter sounds, which take a longer time for babies to pronounce, to be the following:

- **Soft C** (' sé – as in Cease), **CH** (as in Chase), **F** (as in Fly), **GR** (as in Gravy), **J** (as in Jason), **S** (as in Sun), **SH** (as in Show), **ST** (as in Strong), **TH** (as in 'The' or 'Thesis'), **Qu** (as in Quick), **V** (as in Velvet), **X** (as in both 'X-ray' and 'Xylophone'), and **Z** (as in Zipper)

Other letter and vowel sounds (e.g - **L** (as in Yellow), **R** (as in Row), **T** (as in Toe), **Y** (as in Yo-yo) and **Long U** (as in Tube)) seem to fall somewhere in-between the above 2 categories in terms of ease and difficulty.

Many English speaking babies tend to say 'ma-ma' or 'da-da' very early. I wouldn't want to pop any proud parent's bubbles as to whether these words come first out of sheer ease to pronounce or undying parental adoration ...but suffice it to say, '**m**', '**d**', and '**a**' do all happen to fall in "The Zone". If your 4-month baby throws out a random 'ma-ma', you may want to hang on before alerting The Guinness Book Of Records as to the newest, youngest genius.

But, now that we know what letter and vowel sounds lay in and out of "The Zone", we can help construct and introduce certain easier-to-say words and sounds into our little choo-choo's world.

At very early months, while snuggling or playing with baby, let him watch you mouth and say the ZONE sounds. Little monkey can watch you stretch out sounds with your fun cartoony pitches and voices "Ohhhhhhhhhh...Ohhhhhhhhhh... Ohhhhhhhhhhhh.... Aaaaaaaaaahhhh...Aaaaaaaaahhh"... and so on. Even at 4 months, our two little ones would sometimes make the same mouth gestures back, sometimes giving us an "Ooooooooooh"... of course provoking ecstatic praise and kisses. Make it a game everyday... Try singing the Zone sounds "ma ma ma ma ma ma ma ma". But make sure baby watches your lips and mouth.

As time progresses, introduce and focus baby on easy word combinations based on THE ZONE sounds. When you can show or associate objects with the words, even better. When you can hold an object close to your lips so that baby may see your mouth also saying the word, even better.

You can even touch (on your and baby's mouth) where the sounds are made to help baby feel the emphasis placement of the sound. For example, touching the lips for **B** and **P**...or the roof of the mouth for **N**...or the back of the teeth for **T**.

Some speech therapists recommend at times holding a mirror in front of baby so that he can see how his mouth sounds out the letters and words, in comparison to the parent's mouth. Putting stickers or pictures (such as images of balls, family, animals, etc.) on the mirror can also help motivate and excite baby to want to say those particular words.

The words might not come out perfect at first, but they will be much closer than words using letter sounds outside of The Zone. Have fun figuring out what Zone sounds are initially more motivating and exciting to your particular baby, then work on words around those sounds. When they say the word or similar sounding word, remember to praise and encourage, then repeat the correct word back.

Here are some example words incorporating Zone sounds that our babies began with...

"Mama", "Dada", "No No", "More", "Up", "Down", "Ball", "Apple", "Bye Bye", "Car", "Dog", "Baba" (for bottle), "Papa", "Duck", "Ca-Ca", "Toe", "Eye", "Go", "Boo", "Knee", "Pee Pee", "NaNa" (for Banana), "Agua" (for water), "Elmo", "Rrrrrrr", "Mooo", "Bubble"

This is not to say that you only have to use Zone letter sounds to entirely spell a word. If a word contains some of The Zone sounds, it will make life easier for your baby. "Ball" for example may come out as "Ba" for some time until baby is able to say "l". "Woof Woof" may come out as "Woh Woh", until baby can enunciate "f" some months later. But that's perfectly all right. Baby is communicating the object he sees and taking "baby" steps at learning the language. Some words our babies pronounced were at first so off, but so cute, that we started calling a few objects by that word instead. Any sort of cracker was known as a "Bah-m" in our household for months, and we still refuse to call crackers by their real name. Suffice it to say, you probably wouldn't want to make a habit of changing every object to the name the baby gives, but it can be fun to add a couple new words to the English language.

RECAP: Starting baby off on easy-to-say sounds and letters makes it easier for baby to begin speaking. Take time to point out and teach sounds, objects and words incorporating The Zone. Let baby see how your and her mouth shapes the sounds. Touching the mouths to show sound emphasis and incorporating mirrors can also be helpful tricks. Don't worry if the words don't come out perfectly. Just keep encouraging through praise and repetition, and remember to keep it fun. If baby is not enjoying the lesson at hand, move on to something else. You can always revisit a word.

Build Baby Build

Once baby has begun saying certain sounds or words, you can use those to build on new or similar sounding words. Allow baby to take the basics he's learned and apply them to the next level.

For example, suppose little 5-month old Gavin consciously repeats back the sound "Ohhhhhhhhhhhhhh" when you sound-play with him. You may want to guide baby to try new "oh" words such as "No No", "More", or "Open". Or suppose baby has mastered saying "Elmo". In the bath, have fun pointing to his and your "Elbow", and see if baby has an easier time saying that body part. "Ball" could springboard to new words like "Banana" or "Bop". "Boo" could lead to "Buddha"... and so on.

Remember not to give up on introducing other new sounds and words, but keep in mind what they can and already like to say, and use that knowledge as an advantage. When you want to practice working on a new word, start off with what they know to give them the praise and confidence to try something new. For example, suppose little monkey knows how to say "yellow" and "blue," and you would like him to learn the color "purple." Begin by showing him the object in yellow, and have him say "yellow." Then show him the same object or picture in blue and have him repeat "blue". Once he receives the award-winning praise for knowing those two colors, you can move on to trying "purple". If baby does not say "purple" after a few attempts, start back with yellow to build the confidence again... and so on. If baby doesn't end up saying "purple" during that play session, don't worry. See if you can end on something he does know, and come back to "purple" another time. Never push too hard where baby becomes frustrated. I'll say it again and again...keep it fun!

Scaffolding, a building system that slowly shifts responsibility from teacher to student, is a great language tool. We take what baby already knows, then probe and allow baby to discover new ideas or words. A helpful scaffolding method is the open-ended sentence (aka cloze procedures). For example: "This cup is cold. Feel... cold! This cup is warm. Feel...ahhhh... warm.   How about this ice cube? This ice cube is _____?"   Open-ended sentences can be incorporated into all sorts of interactive play, such as singing, books and nursery rhymes.   Suppose baby is familiar with a song you sing daily, and you want baby to join in on the fun.   You can try leaving out the last rhyming word of a line and probe baby to fill in the word.   For example, you sing "Twinkle Twinkle Little Star, How I Wonder What You Are." Then, you sing it again without the last word: "Twinkle Twinkle Little Star, How I Wonder What You _____". If baby doesn't get it at first, you can cue baby by mouthing the "A" in "Are". Eventually, baby will begin to pick up on it and fill in the missing word.   And in time, you can expand to entire lines, choruses, phrases, etc.

RECAP: Build on what baby already knows. See if you can introduce words and sounds based on, or similar to, what baby can already say. Also, during learning and play sessions, try and get baby to say what he already can before throwing out a new word. The confidence of saying what he knows, then receiving praise, will inspire baby to take on that next word. Have fun with open-ended scaffolding and encourage your little one to fill in the missing words or lyrics to songs, books, sentences, and rhymes.

Prop It Up

The environment can be one of your closest friends and tools for teaching baby to speak early. As actors utilize props to perform on stage, babies need endless props to 'perform' speaking. The good thing is, no matter where you go, there are usually plenty of props for baby's daily lessons.

Toys, gadgets, dolls, and other store-bought or hand-made products made specifically for babies come in quite handy for developing motor skills, dexterity, identification, sensory stimulation, and other skills. You may find certain toys to be more helpful in progressing speech. Here are some top recommended 'props':

Picture Books – These are a must. Picture books offer a way for your child to make sense of the world in categories – a key to learning. Gather or create plenty of simple picture books. Picture books with animals, foods, colors, toys, people, instruments, letters, numbers, common objects, body parts, etc....you name it. In the early stages, it helps to keep the pages fairly simple. Books containing one picture per page, with or without text, work great. Pictures with ZONE letter sounds (discussed in *Vowels, Syllables, Sounds and Words To Begin*) are always ideal (dog, ball, etc.), but sometimes not always possible. Try to have picture books with you wherever you go. Repetition is key. Once your baby learns various words or letters, you may even want to create your own picture book with the pictures/names baby can say, and add to it as baby learns new words. Regularly reviewing known pictures/words, along with praise for saying or attempting the words, will help instill feelings of accomplishment and confidence in baby to learn new pictures.

"Baggie Books" are also a fun engaging way for your little bundle to enjoy learning and saying words. These are quick easy 'books' you and baby create by collecting and "bagging" things you find on your adventures. Say, for example, you take baby to the park. Bring a zip baggie, and when something interests him, such as a blade of grass, sand, or a leaf, put it in the bag. You can also add pictures taken at the event, stickers you collected, pictures drawn by baby, or other memorabilia. Then, at home, you and baby could have fun pulling out the homemade, interactive, "baggie book" and reliving the experience. Because the 'props' in the bag are personal to baby, and things he's made a connection with, the excitement and desire to say these objects is heightened. As you and baby collect more of these take home adventures, you can assemble the various bags into a book (e.g. – 3 hole punch the non-zip end of the bags and place in decorated three ring binder). Some other examples of baggie books might include "carnival day", "beach day", "nature walk", "tide pool fun", "sticker store", "scavenger hunt", "grandma's flowers", "grandpa's coin treasures," "family holiday, " or "Elias's 1st birthday party."

Musical Instruments – Fill the home with drums, bongos, shakers, bells, pianos, sound makers, guitars, recorders, rattles, slide whistles, music boxes, chimes, etc. Sound and music makers are attention magnets and, as discussed in **Cartoon Stew, Emotional Glue**, keep baby happy and engaged. Watch how fast a baby stops fussing when you pass your fingers over a simple window chime. When you play with the instruments with baby, work on teaching the names and sounds the instruments make... "Drum...Drum...Drum... (or) ....Boom Boom Boom" as you tap on the drum. "Shake-a-shake-a-shake-a!"..."La La La"... Make up fun sounds that use ZONE letters to go with the instrument. "Bonk...Bonk...Boop... Boop...

Bing…Bing…Pop…Pop… Ring…Ring…"…etc. In no time, baby will be asking you to bring her the "drm drm drm!"

Bath Props: The bath is an ideal environment for teaching baby to speak. You usually have baby's full attention in this relaxed, happy and cozy atmosphere. Get in the bath with your little pumpkin and have fun playing and learning. Some great things to have on hand include a bubble machine, waterproof foam alphabet letters, floaty animals (ducks, frogs, turtles, dolphins, fish, etc.), plastic cups and bottles, boats, floaty rings the same size but all different colors, wind-up water toys, and a toothbrush. Each day you can also work on body parts showing baby (his and your) body parts using methods previously described (fun, animated, repetition, praise, etc)… elbow…knee…nose…lip… eye… toe…ankle…etc. You'll find many body parts have Zone sounds. Water fascinates little ones. Teach action Zone words like "…drip drip drip…up up up…down down down…agua agua agua (foreign languages discussed in *"Mas" Language*)…kick kick kick…etc." Make bubbles with the bubble machine and exclaim "Bubble bubble bubble"…then…"Pop…Pop… Pop!" the bubbles. Have fun sticking foam alphabet letters on the bath…on you…on baby…and practice saying the letters (start with Zone letters first). Be creative.

Colors: For learning to say colors, it's always helpful to start with identical objects of different colors. Let's not confuse baby at first when trying to learn colors by introducing different objects with different colors. Keep it simple during color lessons: same objects, different colors…7 pictures of the same shape having different colors…5 different colored rings for the bath…10 colored rectangle blocks…20 crayons…3 different colored ducks…etc.

Activity Toys: "Ball" is often an early spoken word, usually because 1) how can a baby not be interested in a big fun attention magnet that rolls, bounces, makes silly 'boing' sounds, and is amusing to throw, and 2) it's easy to say (Zone letter sounds). Any object that engages baby and excites her is prime 'prop' material to introduce. Something your monkey can physically touch, suck, play, and fidget with give the words tangible associations and accelerates saying that object (verses just pictures of the object). Some examples might include squeaky ducks, toy cars, talking or activity dolls, pop-up books, teethers, teddy bears, push button toys, noise making toys, toys with lights, spinning and/or motion gadgets, and drawing toys. Of course, being able to interact with actual animals, hear them, feel their textures, etc., is also a wonderful "activity toy" experience. It's good to have a bag of activity toys with you wherever you go (at the doctors, in the car, in restaurants, etc.). Repeated exposure, recognition and play time with the object gives baby the extra push to say the object. And of course, objects with Zone letter names are even more helpful (ball, duck, car, etc.) to encourage baby to speak.

Doodle and Magnetic Drawing Screens: These are also a must have prop; they're great for practicing letters, numbers, pictures, and words (words at later stages). Some screens also allow for drawing in color, which is another perk to practice colors. Once baby begins saying letters, keep a portable drawing screen with you when on the go, and play 'what's this' throughout the day, drawing "A's...B's...C's" for baby to name.

Outside: Babies love to be outside with the trees, grass, leaves, clouds, birds, planes, moon, dogs, bikes, cars, rocks, flowers and other outdoor "props". Take a daily walk with baby along the same route, each time pointing out the same objects. Let baby touch the tree and grass. Let munchkin listen to the sounds the birds, cars and animals make. Have baby touch and repeat back the objects and sounds each day you pass them; in no time, baby will recognize and say these objects as you re-walk the same route. As we learned, with familiarity and enjoyment comes the security and confidence to speak.

Foods: Foods are sometimes the ultimate prop. Once baby can eat real foods (other than milk), you'll find it relatively easy to teach names of foods they like and want. Help baby to speak the name of the snack before giving it to her... "O's...look Aly...O's...Yum... Does Aly want O's?... What do you want?.... Good Aly!...O's...here you go". With this approach (having baby express what she wants to eat), O's, apples, nanas, grapes, carrots, chicken, etc. soon become quick additions to baby's vocabulary.

RECAP: There are endless props to help progress and stimulate baby's speech. Props using the Zone letter sounds, that are also fun for your little one, may be best to introduce first. We've provided some helpful examples above, but don't let that limit your creativity. Learn what types of objects your baby particularly loves. Some little ones gravitate toward electronics, some towards fluffy animals, some towards certain colors, some towards pop-up or baggie books, others towards things that make music. Experiment and bring home more of what baby gravitates toward. Our little one couldn't get enough of electronic gadgets... phones, calculators, car alarm remotes, clocks, remote controls, TVs, stereos, flashlights, etc. Instead of constantly worrying about baby breaking every expensive 'adult' toy in the house, we took a trip down to Radio Shack and picked up an inexpensive set of gadgets just for our little button pushing fanatic. Eventually "mama phone please" turned into "my phone please" and the world was once again in balance.

Sing Sing Sing

Singing and music are necessities in any baby's development. Multiple studies have been published showing the benefits of music in a child's, and even in a fetus' development. Some studies have reported a connection between listening to certain classical music to higher IQ's. Other studies have linked higher math skills to people who played musical instruments at early ages. And other studies have focused on the emotional and behavioral benefits of music during the early stages of life (as well as later stages). But to sum it up: music's great for your baby.

In relation to speech development and progressing through the early stages of talking, music is key. Sing and play music throughout the day…at home…in the car…before bedtime…in the bath…when feeding baby…with family. If you are reading this book before baby is born, sing and play music to baby in the womb. Let baby's world be filled with fun, happy, joyful tunes. As usual, make it fun for baby. Dance around and be silly, use your hands…arms…legs…body. Let baby know that singing and music are fun and should be encouraged. Any songs that allow you to interact with baby, or do physical things while singing, are a major plus. "The Itsy Bitsy Spider", "Skimada-rink-ee-dink-ee-dink", "Twinkle Twinkle Little Star", "Row your Boat", "The Wheels On The Bus", etc.

There are endless audio releases with children's music. It's always good to have a few copies of your favorite cds so you can keep one at home, one in the car, one at the grandparents, and an extra for when baby decides a CD looks like a tasty teething toy. Repetition as we know is key, so don't hold back on repeating songs to baby. Sometimes it also helps to sing at a slower speed without the usual audio recording to help baby learn the parts. The more familiar they are with the songs, the sooner they will begin humorously humming or signing along with the words.

Of course, the "A-B-C" song is a great tune to sing...morning, afternoon and night if possible. The sooner your little munchkin starts recognizing and saying the sounds of the alphabet, the easier it will be to pronounce all sorts of words. So make sure to expose baby to the "A-B-C" song, no matter how much you feel like jumping off a ledge should you hear that tune once more.

You can also have fun making up little sing-song ways of saying words. Throw a little melody under a "no no no" or "ay yi yi!". Pretend the stuffed animals are singing words. It's very cute when you finally ask baby if he wants more water, and he responds "more more more" in a little jingle. Again, like other topics we discussed, be creative and invent new ways of associating music and words.

RECAP: Music makes the "words" go 'round. Spend time every day playing, singing, and exposing baby to the magic of music. Have plenty of music at home, in the car and other places you go, and remember to repeat songs to create recognition and comfort. You might want to avoid Heavy Metal and Gangsta Rap at this point, and stick to happy, fun, silly, baby-friendly tunes...ok, maybe a little Beatles. Have fun making up tunes for words, letters and expressions. The more baby can associate the words to enticing music, pictures, props, etc., the faster baby will begin speaking.

Got Book?

Books are going to be a continual staple and essential element in your child's lifelong growth.   In *Prop It Up*, we discussed the importance of picture books in the early stages of learning, and we suggested some helpful 'picture book' strategies.   But let's look at books and their importance as a whole.   The benefits of reading with your child each day has been advocated in study after study.   Some favor 15 minutes a day, others suggest more book time.   But as a whole, most professionals agree that reading to and with your children is vital.   Many specialists even argue that it is important to start reading to your child during pregnancy, for reasons ranging from recognition of parent's voices, to higher I.Q.'s, to faster understanding and engagement of the spoken language.

The more a child hears and engages language being spoken, read, etc., the better he will pick up on its inflections, pronunciation and dialect, and the sooner he will repeat back the words and phrases. The more emotional and interesting you can make the stories, via tricks we've learned thus far (i.e - your voice, pictures, repetition, playfulness, interaction, scaffolding, etc.), the more baby will want to be involved with the book reading experience.   Be a model for your baby, let him see your love of reading, and remember not to make reading a bore or a chore!

During reading sessions with baby, there are certain things that will help your little angel be even more involved and ultimately want to read out loud.   In the early stages, even before baby can say a word, let baby turn the pages.   Encourage baby to touch and hold the books, and show her how to turn pages when you give her the signal or simply say "turn the page".   There are plenty of books out there with added textures, pop-ups, and interactive pages (pull, squeak, flip, etc.), which are superb for getting baby involved. Encourage baby to touch the many textures and engage the book. Let her learn to love reading.

There are also countless 'non-traditional' books that babies can also experience and read with parents, including magazines, art books, signs, posters, movie ads, travel and nature pamphlets, cereal boxes, food labels, science books, anatomy charts, comic books, traffic signs, song books, and the funny pages, to name a few. Don't feel limited solely to traditional or store-bought children's books.

It's also wonderful for baby, once crawling or walking, to have access to a set of books (usually the more indestructible ones), which she can take out and play with on her own time. This will empower baby, give little one time to "pretend read" (a normal step in learning to read), and allow parents to see what actually interests baby. Have a low book shelf or accessible spot where your little 'monkey' doesn't have to 'climb' to grab her favorite hardbacks.

Also, remember the internet is one humongous, amazing book where parents can pull up and/or print out most anything for children, including read-along sites, sing-along sites, live animals and science exploration sites, endless pictures, art masterpieces, encyclopedias, stories, poetry, interactive learning sites, and much more. One note of caution: there is debate as to when and how long children should be allowed to view and play on computer screens. Many recommend waiting at least until the age of two, and sticking to human interaction as much as possible.

Be creative in finding new sources that will engage and stimulate baby to the wonder of reading and information. Remember to use the techniques discussed so far when reading with baby, but most of all, try to read with your little one each and every day.

RECAP: Somewhat obvious, but important: reading is good. With the chaos of raising a child or even just living daily life, it's sometimes hard for parents to find the time to sit down and read with baby each day. But remember, there are endless sources of reading materials almost everywhere you turn. Books are portable, so if you lead a busy life, find the time to read with baby when waiting for dinner to arrive at the restaurant, in the car ride home, in bed, in the bath, etc.   If you make the extra efforts and get your little one interested and excited about reading early, the benefits, time-saved, and future payoffs will be abundant.

TV Good?

We've heard over and over of the 'evil' and 'wicked' influences of television…the violence, the sex, the cultural brain-washing, materialism, corruption, lies, profanity, etc. It's a wonder anyone is allowed to own a TV! Surely there must be something positive on television. Surely there must be something a little one can watch without turning his brain to mush? Are TV's really just mindless baby sitters for lazy parents?

Well, you're in luck. There are, in fact, some pretty spectacular things on TV that may actually help children to learn, grow and speak. With so many specialized channels, the choices and availability has actually made television a safer and more educational place to visit.

One thing to note is that there are debates on both sides as to the age a child should be allowed to watch television. Some advocate very little limits, while others argue for a complete TV ban. Until concrete proof is found concerning the effects of television on very young children, the American Academy of Pediatrics recommends avoiding TV for children under the age of 2, and not more than one to two hours per day of educational programs after that point. Where you lean on this debate will be a personal decision that only you and your family can make.

However, let's look at some positive destinations and examples we've found if and when you introduce TV:

<u>Nature, Animal and Travel Channels</u> – Sure going on an African safari to witness cheetahs and giraffes in their natural habitat might make a pretty big impact on baby, but it's probably not the first destination trip you'll be taking with your 9-month old. However, flip on the "tele" and you'll most likely find those same animals on an African documentary pretty quickly. There are countless shows and programs with beautiful and up-close images of practically any animal or nature subject. Spend time taking baby into the heart of Asia to see wild elephants and jaguars. Take baby on a scenic flight soaring above the alps or city sky lines. Catch a local tribe performing it's ancient traditional and ceremonial dances. The world is at your fingertips. When you can't travel to the ends of the earth, bring those places, cultures, animals, sights and sounds home to baby. Sit with baby and teach him the words associated with the pictures. At times, you might not even want to turn on the volume. "Birds", 'Monkeys", "Trees", "Ice", "Water", "Seas", "Frogs", "Dogs"... you name it. And now with so many ways to record and playback, once baby becomes interested in a certain topic, such as "Fish", you can also store TV shows on DVR or buy a physical disc, then work on learning through repetition. Just remember to talk and teach baby about what he is seeing using the methods discussed thus far.

<u>Children's Shows</u> – Shows like Sesame Street, Little Einstein, Barney and Blue's Clues are so successful at holding children's attention while at the same time being educational, that millions of dollars have gone into research just to create and imitate the strategies developed by these shows. Focus groups, tests, surveys, experiments, interviews, research, on-air trials and much more go into making what look like simple, innocent children's shows. A great TV series we recommend for babies that has stood the test of time is Sesame Street (and no we are not getting any sort of promotional fee for backing this show).   Sesame Street is simply packed with daily important and wonderful lessons presented in fun, interactive, 'attention magnet', often musical ways that really make learning a pleasure for little ones. Letters, numbers, foods, animals, colors, objects, songs, shapes, sizes and much more come alive through puppets, animation, live action and other techniques that really engage the young audience. With a little parent involvement while watching, repetition of viewing specific lessons, and added props

(i.e. – Elmo doll, etc.), this show can offer great opportunities for teaching baby to speak.

Music Channels – Many broadcast and satellite stations offer 'music-only' listening channels in all sorts of styles and genres. You can always flip on a children's or 50's music station and enjoy singing along with baby.

Reviewing: After watching TV with your little one, it's helpful if possible to follow-up with a prop and further discussion.   For example, suppose you just watched 10 minutes of colorful fish and sea life in the Hawaiian Islands. Bring some fish toys in a bowl of water or the bath, and let your little marine biologist explore first hand the sea. The excitement and interaction of seeing and playing with what they viewed on TV will help pull out those precious words.

RECAP: As we can see, TV might not be all bad. Obviously, excessive TV, no supervision, or the wrong kind of viewing is not recommended for children. As well, there are debates as to the age a child should be allowed to watch television. But a little Sesame Street or the local pet show during a snack might be just the thing to stimulate some new exciting words. You'll find baby will enjoy and react more to the same episode each time he watches. So have the video recorder button ready or simply purchase favorite episodes.

Makes "Sense"

We can use senses similarly to the way we use props or music in order to heighten the learning experience. Senses such as smell, touch, taste, and sound all contribute as added emotional 'glue' to encourage baby to speak.

A picture of an apple is great, but being able to actually touch, smell and taste the apple will better connect baby's senses to the object and, in effect, promote identifying with and saying the object name more quickly. A good example might be flavors of ice cream; imagine trying to teach 'vanilla', 'chocolate' or 'strawberry' to a child without them being able to taste or smell the flavors. The emotional 'glue' would be lost. Let's look at how utilizing some specific senses may help to encourage the speaking experience.

Touch: Even though baby has not fully developed all senses (sight, audio separation, etc.), her sense of touch is pretty strong from day one. As baby grows, she explores her environment a great deal through touch. As you teach saying objects through methods we've already discussed, make sure to let baby hold the objects, feel different textures, enjoy a nice gentle tickle, etc. Let baby experience cold and warm feelings with objects or water while saying words such as "ice," "cool", and "hot." Often her mouth becomes a testing and exploration area for many objects in the first year as motor skills and vision are still developing. Don't be too paranoid about letting baby explore with her mouth, as long as it's sanitary and safe from hazards (lead, poisons, choking, etc). When baby begins teething and wants cool and soothing things to gnaw on, it's a great time to try teaching baby words such as "ice," "cold," "bite" and "cool."

Smell: Did you ever smell something that brought you back to a certain time period or experience? Did you ever buy something just based on smell (cookies, oils, etc)? Did you ever notice what scents make you think of spas and meditation?   Research and marketing have demonstrated that smell is a much more powerful force then some imagine, and may influence life choices and emotions ranging from friend selection, living spaces, and sexual partners to aggression, happiness, hunger, and creative moods to name a few.

Babies often recognize their mothers simply by smell. Needless to say, to smell something is to know it. So let little bundle 'take in' the scent of objects and people you are teaching him to identify...things like flowers, fruits, grass, pets, teddy, mom, dad, poop, the ocean, soap, and the many other things you come across.

Sound: This is a sense we've already discussed (singing, music, instruments, pitches, etc), but helpful to take another look, or should we say another 'listen'. Like smell and touch, sound is another powerful memory trigger. Any time an object may have a sound related to it, let baby hear or experience the sound, such as a barking dog, a bouncing ball, a chirping bird, the sound a flute makes, a ringing telephone, a chime, a train horn, etc. The auditory experience will slap on another layer of 'glue' to get baby speaking the words.

Sight: At first, baby's vision is limited. Babies are born both near-sighted and partially color-blind, and they rely more on other senses such as touch and sound. But as baby develops, she begins to see more colors and distance. In the earlier months, before about 4-6 months, it's helpful to bring objects and people closer to baby. Some researchers suggest using black & white objects and pictures to create a dramatic contrast for baby to more easily identify. However, once baby is about 4-6 months, she should be able to distinguish colors. At the beginning stage of teaching to speak, get up close with baby, make sure your breath is agreeable, and practice sounds while letting baby see how your mouth shapes the respective sounds "oooooooooh...ooooooooooh"... "ahhhhhhhhhhhh" ... "Ma ma ma ma ma"...etc.

Taste: During part of the first year, you won't really be able to do much with this sense. But once your little pumpkin is able to eat solid foods (other than mom's milk or the bottle) you'll be able to have fun adding taste as emotional glue. Similar to smell and sound, let baby taste to better identify and say a particular food...

apple, orange, pear, banana, broccoli, etc. A lemon and orange might appear similar in texture, size, and sometimes smell, but taste is going to certainly set them apart for baby. Just remember to have a camera ready when you introduce baby to lemons!

RECAP: Help baby enjoy experiencing senses attached to words, people, animals and things all around. Smell, touch, taste, sight, and sound all contribute as added identification and emotional 'glue' to get baby speaking the words.

The Waiting Game

Another helpful strategy, yet often painful for parents to carry out, is simply the act of waiting. Whether in an effort to prevent a crying incident or simply acting under the banner of 'undying love', parents often immediately jump to solve any "crisis" or "dilemma" their little one might be experiencing. The second little Timmy makes a discontented sound, appears to want something, or seems restless, new parents often believe if they do not urgently fix the 'emergency' at hand, some sort of permanent psychological damage will occur. We often make ourselves quite batty trying to prevent a baby from crying.

Often parents will even come to know their baby's noises so well that they can tell what the little bundle needs simply by a specific sound or whimper they make. Studies have shown that almost all newborn babies seem to make the same set of sounds when asking for certain basic needs (food, sleep, relieve gas pain, need comfort/swaddling, etc.). This may have evolved from a human survival mechanism in order to aid in infant survival during the early critical months. Many parents either intentionally or unconsciously learn to tap into and identify these survival sounds their babies make. This unique communication can be a wonderful and helpful

interaction for parents and baby in the early months, and is definitely recommended for parents to learn. However, as time proceeds, parents (and baby) may end up relying too heavily on this 'survival' type of communication and might put off moving into the next stage of learning actual language. "I already know Ethan's hungry by that sound he makes, so I'll go get his food" becomes the thought process, instead of trying the waiting game...

Before jumping to your little one's 'urgent' demands, it may be beneficial (once they can consciously construct sounds and words) to wait a second and help him work a little to say what he wants. Obviously if he is in dire danger, this is not a time to wait. As well, doing this too soon or too often may cause unneeded frustration, which can be unhealthy. But let's go back to the Ethan example.

Suppose little 1 year-old Ethan makes his usual 'I'm hungry' nudge sound. It's worked before, so he's sticking to it. Instead of taking the bottle or banana and instinctually popping it into Ethan's mouth, try waiting a second. See if you can 'coax play' him to say the word or something similar to the word. "What's that Ethan? What do you want?" Let Ethan see the mashed banana. "Ohhhhhh...this... banana! You want a banana banana ...[fun smiles by parent]? Can you say banana? OK, let's give Ethan a banana!" While feeding him, make sure to repeat, "Mmmmmm....banana!... Ethan's eating banana!...More banana?" "Oh, do you want more banana? Can you say ba-na-na? You get the point.

For now, it's good to know that useful times to teach language come when your child wants something. Instead of always instantly giving baby what he "urgently needs", whether it's to be picked up, fed, handed a toy, or allowed to pet the puppy, practice the waiting game once in a while. Help him work just a little, with positive encouragement and a fun spirit, to learn the words. It will help your cutie pie understand that she could express through language what she wants. And as your baby begins the stages of talking, the waiting game becomes even more helpful, especially in teaching manners, patience, and how to ask with words such as 'please'.

RECAP: While it may be easier to give baby what he wants simply by knowing you're baby's mannerisms or instinctual sounds, doing so for too long may slow down the talking process.   By six months, it might be beneficial to once in a while incorporate a little waiting.   Waiting and helping baby work to say the things he desires motivates baby to learn language.   Definitely don't be mean about making them wait or cause unneeded frustration, but here and there a little pause to motivate baby to speak can be a helpful tool.

"Mas" Language

With such a culturally diverse society, many babies are born into bilingual or multi-lingual families, or to parents who simply want to teach their children additional languages. Most would agree that learning additional languages is quite beneficial. As well, most findings agree that foreign languages are more easily learned before the age of 5. However, the more languages children learn early, the longer it may take them to speak overall; yet, once they do begin speaking, they will speak in all the languages. So if you are having baby learn multiple languages at once, allow for a little lag time, as compared with other children who solely learn the native language. However, if you incorporate some or all of the techniques discussed in this book, the overall time it takes baby to speak native and foreign languages can often be reduced.

How and exactly when to teach babies second or third languages is debatable. Some studies recommend introducing foreign languages at birth. Other studies recommend waiting till ages 2-3. Some studies recommend each person solely speaking a different language to baby, such as mom speaking English and dad speaking Spanish...or mom and dad both speaking English and the nanny speaking French. Other studies recommend solely speaking the foreign language in the first years, assuming baby will eventually pick up the native language much quicker living in the native land. Some studies recommend both parents speaking both languages. Some studies recommend if parents cannot speak to baby in a foreign language, at least letting baby see/hear foreign television or songs so that baby can see/hear the inflections, tones and styles of a foreign language, which may give him a better ear for learning/speaking that language later in life.

How, if, and when you decide to teach your baby a foreign language is up to you. However, the techniques discussed in this book can easily be applied to teaching multiple languages.

We've found that if a baby sometimes has trouble first learning a useful word in one language (e.g. – the word may be difficult to say, not contain Zone letter sounds, etc.), baby may more easily say the translated word in a foreign language. For example, you may want to first start baby with the translated Spanish word "dedo" verses the English more difficult pronounced word "finger"… or "otro" verses "other"….or "mento" (Italian) verses "chin" … or "agua" verses "water"… or "mano" verses "hand"… or "oui" (pronounced 'we' in French) verses "yes"… or "bobi" verses "grandma"…etc. Have fun looking up and teaching translations of words and objects that are difficult for baby to first say in the native language. Even if you do not plan on teaching baby to be fluent in a foreign language, languages and translations can at least be valuable tools to helping baby identify certain hard-to-say native words. At minimum, it will impress family and friends when baby exclaims "mas agua!"

RECAP: Parents may choose to introduce new languages to their baby in the early years. While there are different methods and times suggested for baby to learn an additional language, incorporating the techniques learned in this book can help to motivate your little one to learn other languages easier and quicker. Even if you choose not to teach baby to be fluent in a 2nd or 3rd language, you can utilize translations in the early stages for difficult-to-pronounce words.

Narrate Life

Whether you choose to use one, five, or all of the techniques suggested in this book, it's important to at least speak to baby. As a narrator might set up scenes, clarify or guide the audience through a story, you will become your baby's first narrator in her life story. Baby will rely on you to learn about the world around her, how things are done, and how words are spoken. In order for baby to understand and learn the language, it's important for her to hear the language being spoken.

Share with baby what you are doing, eating, seeing, hearing, drinking, lifting, pushing, pulling, moving, touching, smelling, petting, tickling, etc. as you take baby through activities of the day. But remember to involve and engage baby in these activities using the various methods learned in this book (e.g. props, singing, emotions, senses, etc). Solely narrating life as 'verbal diarrhea' might lead to baby tuning you out if she is not 'in' the experience. As well, it's helpful in the beginning to keep sentences and phrases short and simple...not necessarily 'Tarzan' simple, but at an appropriate level of understanding.

Recapping the day's events with baby is also a wonderful technique many teachers incorporate into their lessons. For example, "Today Beth went to the zoo. What did Beth see at the zoo? Did Beth see a t..._____ [parent holds up a plastic turtle]...Yes, Beth saw a turtle! [clap]. Beth saw a turtle at the zoo.   Did Beth also see a monkey? [parent might show a picture of a monkey to Beth] Can Beth say monkey? [yeah!] Monkey! ... Did the monkey jump? Did Beth see a monkey jump like this! [parent jumps to add fun] ...Can Beth jump like a monkey? Yeah! Beth is jumping like a monkey! ...Hmmmm...Did Beth also see a lion?   Here's a picture of a lion.

Can Beth say lion? What sound did the lion make? ... Yes, the lion said 'raaaaaaar! Can Beth say 'raaaaaaar' again?..."

Make sure if and when you leave baby with a baby-sitter, family or friend, that they engage and talk to baby (assuming of course baby is not sleeping).   You might also choose to leave a list of activities with the baby-sitter (e.g – read with baby, go for a "talking" walk, sing the A-B-C song, etc).

Also keep in mind, once your little one begins speaking, she will repeat much of what she hears. So, set a positive example for your child.

RECAP: Talk to your little coo-coo, and become the interactive narrator for their new and curious world.

Food For Thought

Teaching a baby to speak goes beyond just the external influences. As the saying goes, "You are what you eat." Most can agree that the foods we eat have a big impact on our daily lives. Behaviors, performance, moods, productivity, creativity, energy, health, fitness, mental capacity and much more can be attributed to what we ingest. Test scores have been found to be higher based simply on what students eat for breakfast. Brain and body functions have been shown to work differently with varying diets. A variety of illnesses and cures have been attributed to intake of certain foods, herbs, antioxidants, toxins, liquids, vitamins and minerals. Proper levels of fatty acids, such as AA and DHA, have been found to directly affect infant brain growth and function.

A person who eats nothing but donuts, fried foods, candy and soda every day is going to feel, behave and most likely function differently than someone who has a more healthy, balanced diet. This same thought process can be applied to our babies. When a new-born is given the right nourishments and intake, the baby grows, reacts, thinks, focuses, learns, feels, and functions better. And when a baby's body, mind and spirit are functioning better, this creates a domino effect on tasks such as learning and speaking. The right foods and nourishment can play an important positive role in baby's speech development. Let's look a little more closely at nutrition and food in relation to certain stages of growth.

(One note of caution before proceeding in this chapter: while we have collected the following information from multiple sources, doctors, research, publications, etc., we recommend always checking with your own doctor regarding any medical or nutritional advice for your baby)

<u>Pregnancy and Breast-Feeding Stages:</u> During these stages, it's important for mom to have a healthy, well-balanced and varied diet. Since baby is dependent on receiving all of it's nutrition from mother during pregnancy and breast-feeding, it's up to mom to consume the right foods, vitamins and nourishments. Factors such as bone development, cognitive functioning (tied to memory and speech), proper oxygen levels in the blood stream, digestion, and general overall health are dependent on the right foods and supplements. It's always advisable to consult with doctors and experts for specific nutritional information and updates. However, as a whole, we've found that most professionals recommend for mother at least by the second or third trimester:

- Prenatal vitamins and folic acid (if possible before mom becomes pregnant)
- Proper amounts of calcium, fiber, protein, iron, carotenoids, vitamin A, antioxidants, folic acid, omega-3, AA and DHA's, and other essential nutrients, vitamins, minerals, and supplements
- A healthy diet rich in fruits, vegetables, and whole grains
- Recommended amounts of protein
- Limiting fats, salts and sugars
- Avoiding harmful things like alcohol, raw seafood, undercooked meat, mercury, unpasteurized foods (such as unpasteurized cheese), and excessive caffeine
- Checking to make sure any prescribed or over-the-counter drugs and/or herbs will not have a negative effect on baby
- Choosing organic over non-organic foods when possible

While we have not found any speech experiments or tests based solely on the above control factors, it does seem logical to assume that these factors would have an influence on baby's learning and speaking processes; after all, a healthier, balanced and well-nourished baby has less health problems to deal with and more time, energy and brain power to focus on the fun of speaking and learning.

<u>Formula and 'Real' Food Stages:</u> If baby is put on a formula, cereal or a supplemental diet before introducing solid foods, make sure to follow doctor's advise as to the proper daily amounts baby should consume based on weight, size and age, as well as which formulas and cereals are optimal (e.g. containing the needed

vitamins, minerals, AA and DHA's, milk or soy, etc.). Obviously, a malnourished or sick baby will have more on her mind than learning to speak.

Once we begin introducing solid foods to baby, many advocate, if possible, stick to natural and organic for optimal health, body and brain function. How much more time does it take to mash up a real banana verses opening up some packaged, shelf-bought jar of baby food? Throwing organic chicken, zucchini, carrots, and other vegetables in a small blender for a soup lunch takes less then 5 minutes, and is a much healthier alternative then grabbing some random canned soup or kid's meal at a fast food chain. In this age of chemicals, pesticides, toxins, hormones, artificial additives, antibiotics, preservatives, sweeteners, and other potentially harmful substances, is it really worth risking baby's health and development during such an early, delicate stage of life?

As with many things in life, whether a car, musical instrument, friend, spouse, or family...the more care, maintenance, and 'nourishment' we put into that 'thing', the higher functioning, performance and 'life' we'll get out of it. Your little one's insides are just as, if not more, important as the societal, educational and other influences outside baby.

RECAP: Teaching your baby to speak also involves monitoring what goes in that little mouth (and body). A healthier baby with the right nutrition, nourishment, and food intake will have more time, energy and brain power to enjoy and learn the process of speaking.

Kid-Nap

No, this is not a chapter on how to kidnap small children for big ransom money. Rather, it's a look at sleep and its influence on your baby learning to talk.

While most times of the day can be fine for baby to learn new words and practice speaking, we've found there can be more optimal times. If little one is cranky, tired, or moody, you're going to find it rather difficult to get him motivated to talk or enjoy learning. When baby rubs his eyes and ears, is fussy, or rubs his face on a bed or parent, it may mean that baby is ready for a nap...not the best time for speaking lessons. It's important not to push baby to speak at these times, but rather 'give it a rest'.

All babies' sleep patterns are a little different, but there are some generalities for the usual amount of time and frequency babies sleep:

- **0 to 1 Month:**   Sleep up to 18 hours a day in short 2–4 hour cycles
- **1-4 Months:**   Sleep up to 15 hours a day in 4–6 hour cycles, more in the evening
- **4-6 Months:**   Sleep 12–15 hours a day, with about 3 naps
- **6-12 Months:**   Sleep 12–15 hours a day, with about 2 naps

- **1-3 Years Old:**   Sleep up to 14 hours a day, with 1 nap

As mentioned, the above are just general guidelines, but they give you an idea as to whether baby is getting enough sleep and is not too sleep-deprived to want to learn.

An optimal time to take advantage of and practice words with baby is after he wakes up and has something to eat. Baby is alert, energized and curious. Other good times baby is usually awake and eager to talk are during snacks/meals (usually sit-down meals verses breast/bottle feeding), bathing, outdoor play, group classes (i.e. – music and mommy-and-me), and play time with friends.

There are optimal awake times when it might be better for baby to just take in information, and not necessarily be expected to repeat back. During bottle or breast feeding, baby can listen to music, singing or reading. Some parents say the only way to get their baby to drink a bottle is to have baby view his favorite TV show while drinking the bottle. If that applies to you, this might be a good awake time to play a fun educational program, such as Sesame Street.

In general, patterns and routines can be positive for babies. They can help baby to feel more secure and safe, which could result in greater confidence to speak, let alone function. Scheduled sleep and nap patterns, although not always easy to make happen, can be helpful as they:

1) prevent baby from becoming overly tired and cranky, making it easier to enjoy and practice learning/speaking;
2) create familiarity and security in a strange world, which builds confidence to face new things (such as speaking);
3) give parents a break to recharge, as raising a newborn and teaching them to speak takes a decent energy toll on mom and dad.

As baby gets older, you may want to set up scheduled times to read to baby before a nap or bedtime. As mentioned above, if baby is fussy and overly tired, you probably don't want to push baby into reading or speaking; but as he gets older, he may look forward to hearing and learning a favorite story, talking or singing a favorite song before sleep. Some research even suggests that students studying or reading before sleep may help to better 'implant' that information in memory as a persons 'sleeps on' the data.

Another area to look at is *where* baby actually sleeps. This is a much debated subject among parents, professionals, doctors, naturalists, psychologists, therapists, and most other "ist's". Whether and when a baby sleeps in a crib or co-sleeps with parents is something you will need to decide. Some warn of the risks of sleeping with parents, such as over-dependency and safety issues, while others boast of the benefits, such as security, nature's intention, ease of feeding, and less exhaustion having to get up at night. How this relates to a baby speaking early is tough to determine, but is something to think about.

RECAP: When and how much sleep baby receives can affect whether she is in the mood to learn to speak. It is recommended not to push your little one to speak when she is tired. Find and take advantage of optimal times baby is wide awake and eager to learn. Some argue that putting baby on routines, including sleep/nap routines, may be helpful. Lastly, where baby sleeps may have an effect, although not yet studied, as to her confidence and security level to take on new learning and speaking experiences.

People Power

Generally, no one is going to love, care for, or give as much attention to your baby as you. However, that does not mean that parents should jump inside a bubble with baby and cut off all communications or help from the outside. And for a great many people, being with baby 100% of the time is not an option. However, for baby to learn many things, including speaking, it's actually helpful to get others involved. As long as you are able to set guidelines, insure safety, and relate your plan/wishes to those who might be with your little munchkin, your baby can benefit in a variety of ways from a little extra 'people power'.

For one thing, a baby is exhausting... with one parent, two parents, or four parents. Having others to help out is often a much needed and valuable asset. Whether it's loving grandparents, siblings, close friends, aunts, a trusted daycare, nannies, or other potential aids, everyone benefits. Parents get a break to recharge and regain some sanity; a refreshed parent will then be able to give and teach baby in a more positive way. Family and friends have a chance to enjoy and take part in this little miracle's growing years... and baby is able to experience and learn from a greater resource pool.

Other people can bring in new and creative ways to work with your baby of which you might not have thought. Yes, you are an amazing parent. Unfortunately, there is a little bad news…you're not perfect. You might not think of every spectacular technique or trick to get baby to recite Shakespeare, let alone talk. It's helpful to share information and ideas with other parents, friends, family, and caretakers. Maybe fill them in on some of the techniques you learned in this book, and see what fun ways they can come up with to work with baby. Maybe see what ideas big sis might have to teach baby to say the alphabet. Try to be open to helpful ideas others may suggest.

Other ways to benefit from 'people power' is to enroll baby in classes. Mommy-and-me, baby gym classes, music classes, and other parent-baby groups are wonderful ways to learn tricks and meet others who have very similar goals and passions, including getting their little ones to communicate and talk. Almost every parent wants his or her child to shine. Most parents are working hard at figuring out how to raise their baby in the best way possible …and they want help. Group classes allow parents to interact and share ideas on the newest things they've learned to help baby grow.

Sometimes, allowing babies to simply play with other babies inspires and brings out new words. Whether it's learning their new best friend's name, or simply a toy that another baby might have brought, babies may react more favorably and openly to other 'creatures' that look, sound, smell and move like they do. Encourage baby to speak out the words she sees with other babies (names, clothing items, toys, body parts, actions, etc.).

In general, your baby may respond differently to different people. Different people bring out and inspire baby in different ways. Perhaps Grandma is great at singing with baby and can get baby to sing along. Maybe big brother is terrific at getting baby to eat and say vegetables. Or perhaps your neighbor has a cute kitten that gets your little one excited enough to say "kitty kitty kitty kitty…" Have fun bringing people you trust and love into baby's life, and you will create new sources of intrigue and discussion for baby.

RECAP: Raising a baby, and teaching him to speak, does not always need to be a solo job. As the saying goes, "It takes a village to raise a baby." Take advantage of the wonderful people you have around you, and be open to ideas and help they might provide. If you don't have people around, join classes and meet other parents. Exchange ideas. Let your little ones experience what others may bring to the table. "People Power" can bring with it many benefits.

Conclusion

Woo-hoo! Now you have a nice bag of techniques and tools to get your little one speaking. As well, you are helping baby to have a positive, fun outlook towards learning. What you teach your little one now will serve as a wonderful foundation for future development and cognitive skills. And to top it off, you are developing a close personal bond with your baby by sharing these intimate interactive activities.

But try not to feel too overwhelmed or think you have to master each of these methods perfectly. Some people may choose to use a few of the techniques in this book. Some may choose to use all. Whatever tricks you do decide to integrate is up to you, but hopefully you've gained some valuable information and skills. Just remember to take a fun and positive approach. It's better to raise a happy, well-balanced, loved, and stress-free baby, than one who is pushed too hard, too fast. Have a good time talking and bonding with baby, and prepare to be wowed!

References / Resources

Many thanks, appreciation and credit is given to those who paved the road to "The Talking Baby". Friends, family, doctors, psychiatrists, psychologists, editors, journalists, fellow parents, linguists, professors, writers, television and talk show creators, song-writers, researchers, educators, health care professionals, and many more influences deserve recognition. We do apologize if we've missed any specific persons or organizations.

Government and Health Organizations/Reports: American Academy of Pediatrics, US Food and Drug Administration, British Nutrition Foundation (BNF), European Society of Pediatric Gastroenterology and Nutrition (EPSGAN), The Food and Agriculture Organization / World Health Organization (FAO/WHO) and the Child Health Foundation.

Web References/Sites/Articles:
www.parenting.com, www.health.state.mn.us, www.boston.com/news/nation/articles, www.artifacting.com, www.britannica.com, www.encyclopedia.com, http://www.kidshealth.org, http://babyparenting.about.com, www.ehow.com, http://www.baby.com, http://www.hhmi.org, http://www.whitehouse.gov ; http://baby.families.com; http://www.huggieshappybaby.com; http://www.speech-language-therapy.com/freebies.htm; http://en.wikipedia.org/wiki/Instructional_scaffolding; http://www.carla.umn.edu/cobaltt/modules/index.html?http://www.carla.umn.edu/cobaltt/modules/strategies/ust.html; http://www.cec.sped.org/AM/Template.cfm?Section=Scaffolding&Template=/TaggedPage/TaggedPageDisplay.cfm&TPLID=24&ContentID=4703; http://www.txsha.org/_pdf/Convention/08Convention/Speaker%20Handouts/Kester,%20Ellen%20Stubbe-Using%20Storybooks%20in%20Intervention.pdf; http://www.ncrel.org/sdrs/areas/issues/students/learning/lr1scaf.htm; http://www.ific.org/publications/brochures/pregnancybroch.cfm; http://www.bellaonline.com; http://www.smartbaby.com.sg; http://www.best-pregnancyhealth.info/diet/; http://home.sanbrunocable.com/~tommywatts03/mod_pron.html; http://pregnancyandbaby.com/pregnancy/baby/The-importance-of-DHA-during-pregnancy-and-breastfeeding-5726.htm; www.mypregnancy.co.in/; http://www.squidoo.com; http://www.

canadianliving.com/family/parenting/top_12_sleep_solutions_
for_parents_of_babies_toddlers_and_preschoolers.php; www.
webmd.com; http://www.webmd.com/sleep-disorders/guide/sleep-
children; http://www.apraxia-kids.org/site/apps/nl/content3.asp?c
=chKMI0PIIsE&b=788447&ct=1212055; http://www.aacinstitute.
org/Resources/ParentsCorner/SharingAndIdeaAlbum/Reading/
070101AdaptingBooks.pdf; http://www.talaris.org/spotlight_tune.htm;
http://www.babycenter.com; http://www.scoop.co.nz/stories/GE0706/
S00091.htm; http://studytips.cramster.com/blog-post-23-9.aspx; http://
kidstvmovies.about.com/od/childrenstvnewsinfo/a/babytvdvd.htm;

Personal Sources and Thanks: Alexandria Sweet, Annette Sweet,
Barbara Smart, Bob Corenson, Cecilia Barinstein, Dinko Tontchev,
Donna Aaronson, Dr. Helen Lederer, Dr. Rachel Kramer, Dr. Sandy
Kagan, Dr. Scott Aaron Sweet, Dr. Tally Silberstein, Eden Sweet,
Hillary Brown, Josh Barinstein, Kathy Corenson, Lillian Barinstein,
Marshall Fenig, Maxwell Sweet, Nancy Johnson, Nathan Barinstein,
Noa Sweet, Norbert Barinstein, Roberta Corwin Robinson, Robin
Sweet, Shaun Moynihan, Skyler Barinstein, Stephanie Fenig, Vicki
Briskman

Magazines: Psychology Today, Parenting, Child Magazine, Parent &
Child Magazine, Parents, The Week, Bottom Line

Classes: My Gym, Music Together, Mommy-And-Me, Encino
Community Center, Center For Music and Young Children, Remo

Books/Authors: The Tipping Point – by Malcolm Gladwell; The
Happiest Baby On The Block – by Harvey Karp, M.D.; What To
Expect The First Year – by Eisenberg, Murkoff, And Hathaway; Your
Baby's First Year –by Steven Pishelov, M.D.; How the Brain Learns:
A Classroom Teacher's Guide & Learning Manual for How The Brain
Learns - Dr. David A. Sousa

Newspapers: Boston Globe, LA Times, New York Times

Television Shows, Documentaries and Networks: Sesame
Street, Little Einsteins, Barney, Blue's Clues, Discovery Channel,
Health Channel, Animal Channel, Biography, PBS, Fast Food Nation,
Dr. Phil, The Oprah Winfrey Show, CNN, 20-20

THE
TALKING BABY

Positive feedback or success stories about how "The Talking Baby" has helped you and your baby is welcome and may be incorporated into future additions. Feel free to email success stories to: info@thetalkingbaby.com

info@thetalkingbaby.com
www.thetalkingbaby.com

Made in the USA
Middletown, DE
06 January 2018